Gentrifying The Plague House

Gentrifying The Plague House

Collection of Poetry

E. Doyle-Gillespie

Apprentice
House Press
Loyola University Maryland

First Edition

Paperback ISBN: 978-1-62720-330-2
Ebook ISBN: 978-1-62720-331-9

Printed in the United States of America

Managing Editor: Kelley Chan
Design: Paige Akins
Promotion Plan: Claire Winterling

Published by Apprentice House Press

Apprentice House Press
Loyola University Maryland
4501 N. Charles Street
Baltimore, MD 21210
410.617.5265
www.ApprenticeHouse.com
info@ApprenticeHouse.com

To Piper, Elaine, Sean, Deborah Briggs, and The Betsy
for taking my writing much more seriously
than I've tended to take it.

Contents

Gentrifying the Plague House

The only thing left in that room
is the fever.
It sits in the corner,
humming to itself,
speaking only Spanish
when it chooses to speak at all.
It squats in the corner,
where there was a crib, maybe,
or where a soldier's cot was
hastily dragged.
It becomes a lugubrious buddha
when I enter the room.
That is when it is slippery
and weighed down
by the faces of children and vagabonds.
But when it shows itself,
and you are the audience,
it is something more like a harpy, yes?
Like something from a Salem headstone?
Something that flits and flaps wildly in that
dingy corner?
It grows wings for you,
because in the presence of the *madre*,
it knows its sins and only wishes to escape.

To Be Trussed Up and Waiting

They will slaughter the goat
when he comes back
from the mountain.
They have tethered it to the tree
and they drink rum
through the passing time
as they wait for him to wind
his way back down the dirt road.
They smoke the tobacco that he
gave to them before
he picked up a twisted branch
to use as a walking stick
and said that he would be
back soon.
"Just a little walk.
Then I will come for the meat."
So, now that he has met
the conquistador who sits
forlorn in heavy armor at the
foot of a shattered castle,
and the slave who still limps
from cutting off the cuffs
on the day of his escape,
he comes down
and they gather their knives.

He will collect the meat
and pay them,
he has explained,
but he must see the severed head.
Times are hard here
and he wants to know that
they have not tried to sell him
the carcass of a
withered dog from
the junk yard on
the other side of the road.

Rites Without Water

We will go there after we
are done spreading her ashes.
It will be as it is and as it was
every night that she taught us
James Baldwin and Eve Ensler
from the half-shell of her mind.
We will let the chill melt out of our cheeks,
and we will drink coffee like Americans –
too much and too hot in cups
so large that they defy the circles of our hands.
We will chalk up hours in this place
waiting for the two communist pensioners
that come to play live bluegrass every Tuesday.
You will recall the chaos of her hair
and the view of the town
that her room's window afforded you.
I will ask you, again, to tell me the stories of where
we have gone on our pilgrimage that day –
the school's rear gate,
the library stairs,
the broken and forlorn gazebo
that beckons from the edge of the woods.
We will drink our coffee in the banjo steam
of this place,
and a grey-bearded Tom Joad will sing defiance
of the wind that is coming down from the mountain,
whipping up the dust outside,
churning itself like Charybdis around this town of ours.

Rapture of the Fish Man

The Fish Man kicked up his legs
that morning.
He slapped his hands on the concrete,
and he called out,
chirping and gurgling with a voice
like cracked glass and dry, wooden splinters.
The Fish Man tried to swim in midair that day -
tried to swim on dry land,
tried to swim through the congregation
of jobless, white t-shirts.
He bashed his head down on
the concrete of McMechen Street
and let his red flowers spread across the sidewalk.
The Fish Man, dancing as though
he'd been hauled out of the sea
and on to the deck of a schooner,
christened the street with the foam
and the spit that welled out of him
after he jammed a speedball
into the big vein of his right leg.
He christened the street
with his blood and his spit
until a blond medic,
close to the end of her shift,
came with naloxone to stick
up his nose and wash him
free of his holy ghost.

Conjuring Manzanar

She has an obsession with bodies
in motion, she says.
I listen to her, drink,
and wonder, for a moment,
from the landscape of her face
and the burnished desert of her skin,
whether she is from the First Nations
people that live just beyond this stretch of road.
In this heat, she wears the short boots
and tight, black jeans of the book store girls
I knew in Brooklyn.
She wears a man's tank-top and does her work
through the lens of a 1943 Kodak Brownie
that she took from her dead mother's attic.
When she found the black-box camera,
it was full of her family
– tiny sepia-negative Nisei shop owners,
disappeared into a wasteland like this one.
Vanishing like *yurei*
walking through a solid wall.
And because the camera belongs to her now,
she takes it to the empty spaces
where the sand is still drunk
with the rust of barbed wire.

She takes photographs of the mountains,
the desert floor,
a white obelisk,
and a guard tower,
saying that one day she will put them in a book
about what grows in places where the disappeared
are sent to find their new names.

Excluding the Coldness of My Room and the Strange Ways of Fathers

When I write this,
I will say that the house
was narrow and that it overflowed
with books whose backs were
well-broken by the hands of
old men.
I will say that he
spoke to me
in so many languages that
my teachers feared
for the sanity of my tongue.
In my story,
you bickered with him using
the immigrant mouths of my grandparents,
because the things of which you spoke
were only the business of adults.
I will write that you took me into the
cauldron of our kitchen along
with my sister and the aunties of your coven.
Garlic would cleanse,
I will say you said,
and red wine forgive
if you forget to find it the coolest
recesses of the house.

And I will write that you were working with
the crank of an ancient grinder,
or even a mortar and pestle,
when you explained to me that paprika could be
almost tasteless
if done the wrong way.
If you did not crush the right pepper
in the right way,
it would give you its color,
maybe a trail of its scent,
but when you went to meet it,
 its flavor would only be
a ghost haunting whatever
was meant to bring you sustenance.

The Memory of Fabric

Because she has taken a job
as a waiter in the new place
down the street,
she must dress like James Dean.
It is made up like a 50's drive-in,
and all of the staff must pretend to
be greasers and juvenile delinquents.
She must draw her hair back,
curl it and twist it in a
slick of gel so that it glistens
under the track lighting.
She must roll up
the cuffs of her jeans.
She must chew gum.
I want her to wear my white t-shirts,
though her arms are thicker than mine
and her back broader.
She says that she would,
but she must be crisp for this place.
Her shirts cannot have leaned cluelessly
over the dying entrails of my brother's car,
or spent hours soaking up the smells of the bodega
and the used book stores on 3rd Avenue.
So, I will buy fresh shirts for her,
and she will swirl her hair in the
peaks and canyons that they require.

I will watch from my place at
the kitchen table
as she laces up the black high-top sneakers,
and I will ignore her exhalations
and the crop of sweat that
sprouts fresh and glistens
on the back of her neck.

Cretion Myth in One Day

There are Cuban men in the lobby now.
They have come in the height of the heat
of the day,
in dark designer suits and open collars.
They have come to play chess,
teaching leaps and slanted lines
to young girlfriends,
talking to the Haitian woman
who brews the coffee,
coolly racing from the cigar shop
around the corner to the library chill
of this marble hotel.
And when the sun is swallowed up,
new ones rise out of the Atlantic,
out of the beach's raked sand.
They wear the white pants of cane cutters—
deliberately out-at-the-knee—
embracing conga drums with
sinewy legs as they sit
beside the lobby door.

As I ply the Haitian woman
for another cup,
they thrum the taut hides
of their drums
and they wail their words
because the songs are
ancient loves,
circles drawn in sands,
and an ocean full of dancing bones.

Lilith in Transit

I saw one of Rossetti's "stunners"
on the bus this morning.
I'm pretty sure it was Lilith,
but don't hold me to that.
I mean, she had those Cornforth lips,
and she was brushing her hair,
admiring her reflection in the
mullion's fractured steel,
but I could be wrong.
I folded my paper,
slumped in my seat,
and watched
my commuter Lilith
preen her thick, red curls
as we shuddered past
Holliday Street,
and the old, boarded-up porno shop.
Over her shoulder,
I could see the place where
Clara used to dance on her pole,
and I swear the blind man
on the corner of
President and Baltimore –
doomsday soothsayer
with his all-seeing eye dog-
hailed her as we passed.

But my Lilith,
incendiary in her
Affliction t-shirt,
two rows up,
only twisted her hair
in those tortoise-shell coils,
pursed her lips,
and waited for the
next stop to arrive.

Gossips

The Gossips sit down by the ocean
and work out the knots
that strangle the fishing lines
of their men.
They sit by the sea and wait for husbands
in ancient creaking boats
to come back from the hunt.
The Gossips think that I don't understand them.
I could not possibly
wrap my mouth around their tongue,
and own their words.
This is why they talk out loud
when I go to the market,
or walk down to
the sea to photograph leathery fishermen
and creaking hulks.
They talk about you.
The Gossips say that your father must have been
a black sailor
from one of those British freighters
that came years ago.
That's why your lips are full,
and your hair falls in tight ringlets when you
set it loose.
The Gossips say that you got those bangles
that you wear
from another woman's husband.

When they come to clean my room,
and take away the trays,
they can smell a musk
that could only be from you.
They say that my constant scratching
in my notebook could only be about you.
The Gossips say that I must have a woman
back in America – in Chicago or New York –
but that I have stranded myself on this rocky shore
because you are a nereid,
and I am as helpless as any man
who comes up from the sea.

Much Later, She Will Edit This

If you see the typewriter woman
come down, it will be to buy
our *longaniza* and the fried cheese
that goes with her wine.
And our coffee.
She said once that she could drink
what we brew here,
what we press here,
because she learned about coffee
from her Damascus father.
She was tiny, and he
gave her sips and spoons
as he wrote with his tall script
in the margins
of a second-hand book,
or scribbled on the edges of
beveled pages.
You may see her in men's clothes
talking to the cappuccino women
that cook here,
that carry our kitchen smells
and our butane heat home
in their skin every night.
She came to them on the day
that she finally cleaned out
her father's apartment.

She came with her arms full
of an antique Underwood
and she begged them to
speak at her in unbroken torrents
of coffee-ground Espanish
and wax-paper cooking oil,
until her mourning time was done
and the keys to the new place
were properly blessed.

Vixen in the Alley on New Year's Eve

To show me what she means,
what I must understand,
she rises up on one foot,
stretches one thigh open
and away from its mate -
stands *ecce homo*
in platform heels.
She tells me again that
she has named herself Vixen
and that she is the only white
girl at the Diamond Club
who has no Baltimore stigmata
on the hollows of her arms –
who does not have sleep
shuddering the purple lids
of her eyes.
She is thick and she is healthy,
she tells me again.
She should be the one
to dance for me
because tonight is the first of the year,
and she can tell that
I have chosen the wrong words far too many times.
I have accepted far too much smoke
that has only strangled me.

I have left far too much shredded,
green glass in my wake.
But none of this matters
to Vixen in her platform shoes.
She will forgive me
my trespasses,
she says,
because this is the first of the year,
the horse-back cops are
traversing in front of Eddie's
like a fascist promenade,
and she is the one
meant to usher me inside.

The Last Photo from that Series

For Alex

There were 25 Chicano men standing
like cordwood
in the back of Lester's pick-up truck that day.
There were 25 day-work men that wore gloves made of
callous on their shapeless hands,
wore flannel layers that smelt of sweat,
and stood packed like upright slave ship cargo
traveling on the road that day.
And they all cried out when they saw you
stretched in the kudzu,
laid out by the side of the asphalt ribbon.
They cried out, beat the metal hide of the truck
with those torture-hardened fists,
and cursed the driver to turn around and go back.
They begged the driver to go back to you
 because this was the day that I had asked you to lay
yourself down on the shoulder of that unnamed road.

I had photographed you with cacti,
with boulders,
in dry river beds,
and now I had loaded my camera,
and stretched you out
by that road,
gravid, half-nude
in the early morning haze
so that your hair formed
a web around your face
and the dome of your belly mimicked the
mountain that rose just beyond the bean fields.
I would photograph you this way,
we had decided the night before,
and then we would go to town to
have the *chorizo* breakfast that
we had promised ourselves for days.
And now, 25 Chicano men were cursing
their day-work benefactor
to turn his truck around
because all they could see
was that you were pregnant,
as helpless as an Aztec sacrifice,
and they could not let you have
your baby in a place
as wild and haunted this.

Patriarch

Did you trade my father
ghost for ghost?
When he crouched by the roadside,
sleepless in the furnace of the Mekong Delta,
and you attached yourself to him,
did you trade places with
the pendulum man that he brought
from his home?
You must have, because dad came back
with you, and the French soldier
who burned in my mother's garden
from night to night.
He came back with you
and the pleading rice farmer
and the legless man who floated
past the foot of my bed.
So, Viet ghost, I have to imagine that
your village can smell the kerosene of midnight crosses,
and that a sharecropper swings
from the upper limbs
of some ancient tamarind tree
in the in-between hours
when the sun rises and burns
away the morning haze.

Chasing Zoraster

Tonight, you decided,
we would drink the whiskey
from your bookshelf.
You would tell me
about The Farsi Man
and how you broke your bones
for him.
"The Farsi Man" –
that was what you called him.
That was his name on the nights
that he muttered to you about
the war between evil Ahriman
and his golden brother Ahura Mazda.
That was his name when he
told you to dance in the circle
of his corner table.
You wore only leather biker boots,
and when you fell
and fell again,
he would remind you that
Ahriman would finally lose
to his brother
but that the Earth would have to shudder,
its womb would be ripped open too soon,
and you would realize that creation
is the cruelest trick of all.

The Pele Allowance

You had a lover who ate fire.
Who painted her face
in oily black-and-red,
and wore a second-skin
that made her look like the pyre of
a rioter's rage each time she moved.
She would go to the corner of this or that street
when the midday men broke free,
and she would twirl herself
with her head canted back.
She would catch glimpses and slices
of the red-brick canyon
in her fractured vision,
and the men would become statues for her.
She would take torches into her mouth
and they would fall in love with her.
She would spit her napalm over their heads,
and they would follow
the wake of her ashes,
taking crisply-folded bills from
tailored pockets.

Your lover would spin herself
in a cloak of dreadlocks,
fling fragments of fire into the air
like a dervish majorette,
and the men would search fruitlessly
for the plastic bucket
or the worn top hat
in which to lay
their tributes.

The Adventures of Patience and Fortitude

By the end of the story, the Boricua girl could fly.
She could actually fly.
It wasn't just a controlled fall like in the first chapter
when she surprised the creeping man behind her tenement,
and it wasn't merely attaching herself to the wind,
like when she floated away and landed
on the steps of the 5th Avenue library
in the middle of the night.
By the end of the story, she could crouch
on the ledge of her window,
stretch her body away from the endless noise
of her family's apartment, and just fly.
Now, she could go on adventures with the
Khmer girl who lived two floors down.
She was the one who could turn herself to stone.
Sometimes, she would do just a foot or a fist,
like when she used *bakator* boxing to fight the
corner boys and the thieves who came to raid her
family's store just before closing.
When she needed to, she could make herself
into a sarsen, smooth and the color of egg yolk.
She saved this for when the boys made a ring around her,
wrapping their fists with belts and
the stolen chains of bicycles.
By the end of the story,
the *boricua* girl could fly down two flights,
take the Khmer boxer by the wrist and soar
the two of them off to find danger.

They would be good partners,
she thought.
They both knew the city well,
so there would be few places for
villains to hide,
and this girl who could make herself
into concrete could keep our heroine
from flying too close to the sun.

In the Manner of Hephaestus

First, I decide,
I must make a *makiwara* for her.
The wood – the board –
should have drifted in
from the ocean.
It should be stout –
maybe a beam torn from the ribcage
of a whaling vessel that rolled over
in its sleep and died in the sea
that surrounds our home.
I will haul it up from the beach,
cutting my hands,
baptizing its grain
with a new finish
as I pull it into our yard.
I will wrap it in the coarsest rope
that Chelsea's Hardware has to offer,
and while I made those ouroboros coils,
I will wonder whether
she should knit her hair into dreadlocks
when the time comes.
They would look fierce framing her face,
but then I remind myself
that you must never give them
anything of yours that they can grab
and be used to hoist you from your feet,
or slam you to the earth.

Better that her hair should huddle close
to her skull and that sweat should
bead on her scalp
as she breaks her bones
against the *makiwara's* hide.
And if her eyes fill with watery pain,
I will remind her that
the spider webs that she feels
cutting their way through her bones
are the meaning
of all this.
That they cannot break a girl
who has already fractured herself
against a driftwood *makiwara*.
That Ares was the only father an Amazon
would claim.

Bruja

I asked her to cast the spell again,
this time, closer to home,
and she did.
Instead of recreating the London bistro
for me, she chose the abandoned storefront
six blocks down – the one we pass
during our Sunday walks.
We heard it was a furniture store once,
and then a place for Leviticus voodoo
and Holy-Roller magic.
Now, bare metal tendrils reach down
from the ceiling's dark gape,
glinting at us through
the fractured picture window.
She closed her eyes
and breathed in deep.
She conjured a marble bar,
because I loved that so much
the last time,
and brass rails the color of honey.
She curved the night up
like her in a red dress
with curls sweeping
and Satchmo's version of
Mack the Knife piped in
Deus Ex Machina.

And me? For me,
she materialized the smoldering body
of a thick, brown Cuban cigar
between my index and middle fingers.
She decided I would wear the same blue blazer,
but my shirt would be open at the collar.
As I blew life into the smolder and the reek,
she leaned in the doorway behind me.
She leaned like a teacher
down beside me
as the gloaming poured itself
through the wide window,
and she asked me whether this
was exactly what I meant.

When it was Sanctuary

Time will pass, I tell her,
and they will tear this house down.
They will use guileless hammers
and feral machines to shatter its eyes
and spill it, brick by brick, into
the Gold Street alleyway.
This is how they will find out
that she wrote every night
in a dollar-store composition book,
and that she tended to the shadow people
with nubbin pencils and those precious gel pens
that she hoards.
I tell her to explain how, sometimes,
shadow people passed through
the living room walls,
even on midsummer afternoons
when we ate our dinner on trays,
watching Star Trek,
and tuning out the Baltimore cacophony
of our dead-beat street.
I hope she describes how they came
up through the floor of the bathroom
when her sister was preparing for her date
with that guy who wore a galaxy of gold
across his fists.

I watch her draw one, then two of them
in the rough-edged, smudged way
of sketch-artist girls
and then seal her book
in the upstairs crawlspace.
That is the part of the house that will cave
in on itself last when they knock the legs out
from under this place
and send the walls down to meet the earth.

Acknowledgements

Born from seven poems written over seven days in the library of the Betsy Hotel in Miami Beach, Florida, this book came to its final fruition in the midst of quarantine and social upheaval. I had only a vague notion of what COVID-19 was when I sat down in the library off the Betsy to work as its Poet-in-Residence. There had been fiery debate about my chosen profession as a police officer for quite some time, but the fiery crescendo surrounding the murder of George Floyd was a thing of the future.

Written for the America that it inherited, Gentrifying the Plague House discusses issues of social justice, and cultural space. As the poems formed themselves, they asked me to explore my family's somewhat cryptic Afro-Cuban heritage, the plight of the culturally unmoored. They asked what it means to live in a cultural crossroads and to learn to find an identity in that shadow land. They wanted to discuss isolation and the beauty in the ways that broken communities learn to limp on. It I found my poems, as they shaped themselves, honoring my love of magical realism, myth, and mythology. It was a time to converse in lost languages and ancient tongues.

About the Author

E. Doyle-Gillespie is a Baltimore City Police officer. A 15-year veteran of the force, he has worked in patrol, operations, and education among other specializations. His books of poetry include *Masala Tea and Oranges, On the Later Addition of Sancho Panza, Socorro Prophecy,* and *Aerial Act.* He is a former teacher who holds a BA in History from George Washington University, and a Master of Liberal Arts from Johns Hopkins University.

Apprentice
House Press
Loyola University Maryland

Apprentice House is the country's only campus-based, student-staffed book publishing company. Directed by professors and industry professionals, it is a nonprofit activity of the Communication Department at Loyola University Maryland.

Using state-of-the-art technology and an experiential learning model of education, Apprentice House publishes books in untraditional ways. This dual responsibility as publishers and educators creates an unprecedented collaborative environment among faculty and students, while teaching tomorrow's editors, designers, and marketers.

Outside of class, progress on book projects is carried forth by the AH Book Publishing Club, a co-curricular campus organization supported by Loyola University Maryland's Office of Student Activities.

Eclectic and provocative, Apprentice House titles intend to entertain as well as spark dialogue on a variety of topics. Financial contributions to sustain the press's work are welcomed. Contributions are tax deductible to the fullest extent allowed by the IRS.

To learn more about Apprentice House books or to obtain submission guidelines, please visit www.apprenticehouse.com.

Apprentice House
Communication Department
Loyola University Maryland
4501 N. Charles Street
Baltimore, MD 21210
Ph: 410-617-5265
info@apprenticehouse.com • www.apprenticehouse.com